A TRILLION FACETS OF LIGHT

Poetry and Reflections for Self-Love, Courage, and Dreaming Big

SARA CHRISTIANSEN JEFFS

for Dave, Benj, and Daisy—the great loves of my life

Published by Central Avenue Poetry, an imprint of Central Avenue Marketing Ltd.
centralavenuepublishing.com

A TRILLION FACETS OF LIGHT

Trade Paperback: 978-1-77168-473-6
Ebook: 978-1-77168-474-3

Printed in the United States of America

1. POETRY / Women Authors 2. POETRY / Family

1 3 5 7 9 10 8 6 4 2

CONTENTS

In case no one told you today, you make this world brighter just by being you.

Dear beautiful friend,

There are many things I'm not sure of, but this I believe: If this book ended up in your hands, it was meant to find you.

The truth is, you will probably have already absorbed hundreds, if not thousands, of pieces of information today, but most likely few to none of those messages reminded you of your inherent worth, exactly as you are in this moment. In a world that emphasizes comparison, perfectionism, and endless striving to be more and to have more, I believe this message of worthiness—and the power of our inner light—is essential for our health and happiness. Because when we fully recognize the value we hold, it becomes the foundation for self-love and healing, and empowers us to move forward to the future that is waiting for us.

I've spent over twenty years as a health and wellness professional, and my favorite part of my career is the one-on-one connection. I've had the privilege of hearing thousands of personal stories of incredible challenges, pain, trauma, and hardship. And with those stories, what stands out again and again is the incredible courage, strength, resilience, and wisdom it takes not only to survive those difficulties, but to emerge on the other side with deeper compassion and purpose. It's so important for us individually and collectively to pause, to remember, and to celebrate everything we've overcome and everything that is beautiful and brave about us.

This book shares parts of my own journey, alongside reminders and reflections written just for you. I hope the words on these pages remind you that your inner light—all of the things that make you uniquely you—is immense, multifaceted, and can never be taken from you. I hope they remind you of your courage and inspire you to keep being brave. And I hope you feel empowered to trust your inner wisdom and keep pursuing everything you're dreaming of. Because this world needs you, and the light you shine on it, now more than ever.

Rooting for you always, and deeply grateful that you're here,

Sara Christiansen Jeffs

I.

LIGHT THAT SHINES INFINITELY

Lucky You

You are not a beige aesthetic—
polished and palatable.
You are not a one-hit wonder
with one chance to shine.
You are not a full stop,
a chapter, a single grain of sand,
an expendable object,
a verdict,
a judgment,
a low moment,
a second choice,
or a reflection of another's unwillingness to see you.

You are a million, no, a *trillion*
facets of light.
You are something to behold,
you are permission to evolve,
you are limitless potential,
you are your dreams' safest keeper,
you are off-the-charts altitudes
and larger-than-life multitudes,
and you get to choose you,
get to be you,
get to know you,
get to love you—
how lucky are you?

The Only Permission You Need

I hope you give yourself permission
to live fully without apology
to take up every luminous molecule of space
    you are deserving of
to love and to receive love
to be kind and to receive kindness
to hope relentlessly
    and to forgive yourself when you lose hope completely
to make mistakes
to stumble and get up again and repeat
to dream
to grow
to fall at your own feet
to take your breath away with your power and tenderness
to be anchored in your life, yet never bound by it
to heal in a way that astounds you
to see yourself in the stars
to inhale the night sky
    and to hold the moon at your fingertips
    and then release
to trust
to go back if you need to but not to linger there
to exhale
to feel your beautiful heart beating
to know you are whole.

Your worth is not dependent on your productivity,
your failures or successes,
whether or not the love you give is reciprocated,
other people's validation, expectation, or opinion of you,
or the challenges you're facing.

Your worth is inherent,
unconditional,
as big as the ocean and infinite as the stars,
and can never be taken from you.
It has always been and always will be
woven into the essence of you,
and it is abundantly enough,
exactly as you are in this moment.

Breathe in:

I am grounded and safe in my unconditional worth.

Breathe out:

I am deserving of love, compassion, and acceptance, exactly as I am.

There are people you haven't met yet who will remind you of what love is.

There is healing ahead for the parts of you that need tenderness and care.

There are memories to be made that will make your heart feel safe.

There are adventures to be had that will bring out the child in you.

There are doors to be opened that you're dreaming of now.

Your story is so far from over.

You have survived every hard day,
every heartbreak,
and every moment you thought would break you.
You are living proof that courage exists.

I Hope You Celebrate

The courage it's taken to show up when you had every reason to give up.

The strength it's taken to rise from the ashes of pain, fear, and heartbreak.

The vision it's taken to keep dreaming your big dreams when all hope felt lost.

The fortitude it's taken to rebuild the life you knew you deserved from the start.

The fierceness it's taken to shake up everything that felt safe and familiar because you knew there was something more true and aligned.

The imagination it's taken to believe in a future beyond the discouragement you felt in the moment.

The authenticity it's taken to live as your true self.

The love it's taken to see the beauty all around you and within you.

In Case No One Told You Today

Your worth isn't up for debate—
it's infinite, written in the stars,
and never gets to be determined
by anyone else.

All of the love you've given
is making its way back to you
in a million different ways.

That dream you put on hold
because life got in the way,
that's calling to you now,
is worthy of being heard.

Courage and fear can exist
at the same time,
but when you tip the scale toward courage,
that's when the magic happens.

Your pursuit of growth
is a beautiful thing,
but you are still abundantly enough
right here and now.

You are worthy of living a beautiful life.

You are worthy of being loved fully and unconditionally.

You are worthy of deep and lasting healing
that leaves you in awe of how far you've come,
and joy that lifts the heaviness and refreshes your soul.

You are worthy of celebrating every step
that's brought you to this day.

You are worthy of growth and evolution that expand
your horizons and your vision.

You are worthy of following every dream in your heart.

Repeat after me:

There is nothing I need to do,
perform, achieve, or succeed at
to make me any more worthy
than I am right here in this moment.

I don't know exactly when it happens, but somewhere along the way we absorb messages about who we're supposed to be—for love, for acceptance, and for belonging.

And it takes a certain kind of enlightenment to recognize the learned parts of you that don't serve your growth and alignment.

It takes a certain kind of bravery to shed those parts and return to who you innately are.

It takes a certain kind of strength to rebuild from the foundation upward with the pillars, intentions, and grand design of what you want your life to be.

But it's all worth it. The peace, freedom, and empowerment that come from living an authentic life, one that's ever evolving and growing, is irreplaceable.

Irreplaceable like your unique light.

Irreplaceable like your spirit and who you've always been.

Irreplaceable like the exact blueprint only you hold.

May you have the wisdom and courage to live as you were always meant to be.

And may you feel love surrounding you with every step you take.

Self-love starts with acknowledging your wholeness. It's dispelling the notion that you are broken, or not enough, or that there are parts of you that are unlovable.

It's embracing every part of you—your strengths and weaknesses, your light and your shadows, your courage and your fear.

It's shedding the skin that no longer fits and bravely making room for a life aligned with your values, your passions, and your purpose.

It's knowing in your bones that there is just one of you in this universe, and that there is no better time than now to show up as your true and beautiful self.

Life Force

You don't have to be the life of the party,
shimmering and favored,
dazzling,
influential.
You can be the one in the corner,
the one who remembers the stranger three years later
who told you their dreams
and how they missed their sister,
and how scared they felt of disappointing anyone,
especially themselves.
You can be the one who thinks of them
from time to time and wonders,
Did they become everything they wanted to be?
Did they know they didn't need
to become anything more at all?
You can be the one who marvels
at one life at a time,
who asks,
who listens,
who sees.
You can be the one who marvels
at your own life,
who knows that being interested
makes you more than interesting—
it's light in action.
You can be the one who's certain
that you don't have to be
anything other than you are,
who knows that stranger remembers you too.

And Now for My Next Trick

The one where I stop
disappearing altogether,
put on the biggest top hat I can find,
throw away the magic wand
and put my hands on my heart instead,
turn the lights back on in the neglected corners of the room,
exhale,
release,
embrace the long-forgotten mischief and desire,
go outside,
and dance barefoot under the moon
with every version of me.

Organic Growth

I won't promise you shortcuts
or cheat codes on this healing journey,
no hidden treasures
to unlock a painless path.
But I do know this—
you have a heart that's good,
a soul that everglows,
wounds that when tended to
can beautifully mend,
and a future that's alive and waiting for you.
I hope today you find
the wisdom in this valley
and a glimpse of the joy that returns
after the breaking,
and I hope it gives you the strength
to keep standing firm in the truth
of who you are
as you venture into all that's to come.

You Deserve the Kind of Love That

keeps your heart safe

believes in your dreams

gives you space to grow and evolve

cheers for your wins and sits with you in your losses

reminds you of your light when you forget

and sees you, knows you, and celebrates you.

You deserve to give yourself that kind of love too.

How Does She Love Herself? Let Her Count the Ways . . .

Because she spent what felt like
endless, countless days
shrinking herself down
and picking her apart,
not seeing all the beauty
that she had within her heart.

Letting them decide what she was worth,
accepting verdicts that they gave,
not knowing that their harmful words
reflected their own pain.

She loves her for her courage
and all the times she took a step,
even though she felt afraid
and could hardly catch her breath.

She loves her for her beauty,
the blueprint deep inside
that radiates through everything
and lights the darkest night.

She loves her for her wisdom
that she gained through all the lows,
but she didn't let life keep her down—
she healed and grew and rose.

She loves her for her future,
for her past, and here and now,
she loves her for the way she's learned
what true joy is about.

She loves her for the space she gives
to let her feel it all.
She loves her for the grace she gives
if she ever has a fall.

She loves her for her power
to heal and to forgive,
to walk her path authentically,
to live and to let live.

She loves her for the times that she
forgets to love herself,
and knows she'll find her way again
because she trusts her well.

Anatomy of Goodness

When my children were little
I was determined to teach them medical terms
because I thought they'd need to know one day.
Their little toddler voices would echo mine—
patella
humerus
phalanges
sternum.
It was a cute party trick,
a memorable talent,
but mostly
an assurance for the future.
I wanted them to know that their bones were good.
I wanted them to know in their bones that *they* were good,
and to never let anyone make them believe differently.

All Welcome

Your anxiety / your fear / your heartbreak / your sorrow / your biggest regrets / your messiness / your imperfections / your shadows / your whole entire beautiful heart.

You've been hurt, you've been in pain,
you've felt the thunder and the rain,
but you're living brave,
showing up each day,
holding on to hope and love and light
even when you feel afraid.
That's why they say
not all heroes wear capes—

and you're my hero.

Some days are for resting

Some days are for healing

Some days are for dreaming

Some days are for feeling

Some days are for quitting

Some days are for trying

Some days are for learning

Some days are for flying

Each day is for loving yourself
through the highs and through the lows,

and each day is for remembering
it takes all of the seasons to grow.

I hope you remember to stop for a minute and look at how far you've come—your courage, your strength, the challenges you've faced, and the brave steps you've taken. I hope you remember to celebrate how you're here today, still shining, still growing, still learning and unlearning and dreaming. Little you would be amazed at the battles you've won, the victories you've achieved, and the fierce love in your heart that grows day by day.

II.

LIGHT THAT GLOWS IN THE DARK

A Flickering Light Is Still a Light

There is an infinity to you that's difficult for the human mind to fully grasp. But your very presence, every facet that makes you who you are, and the heart of your humanity, can never truly be dimmed. There may be times you've walked in valleys so dark there was no chance of seeing the horizon. There might be people who hurt you so deeply, and the pain obscured your soul so much, you didn't know how you'd ever find yourself again. But your light was always there. Your light is within you now. And your light will always be there, no matter what.

When the night fell
and light slipped away
and she didn't have the strength
to fight for hope to stay,

hope never let go of her,
love gave her shelter,
clarity replaced the blur,

and she miraculously endured.

Dear Beautiful Human,

If you feel a little lost and alone,
and the way forward's uncertain
and you can't seem to find your way home,
please know the darkest hour
is right before the dawn,
and please know the still of night
is followed by the morning's song.
I'm sending you so much love right now
in all you're going through,
please keep hanging on—
because this world needs you.

It's incredibly brave the way
you look for the light
even when the darkness
feels overwhelming.

Conversations with Friends

Love said, “Go.
You’re free to simply be.
I’m right with you through thick and thin.
I’m never going to leave.”

Fear said, “I’m here.
It’s hard, and that’s okay.
But I’ll be your companion,
don’t hide me away.”

Hope said, “Look,
just a little more in front,
the clouds are shifting quickly,
making way for the sun.”

Wonder said, “Stop
and see this lovely flower?
It started with a seed
and now it’s growing hour by hour.”

Pain said, “Listen,
I’m only here to teach,
but I will not stay forever,
the end is within reach.”

Joy said, “Remember
how you felt when you were five?
There’s so much comfort I can give
if you just let me revive.”

Healing said, "I'm for you
and I promise you I'm real.
There's not a wound that I can't reach,
just keep letting yourself feel."

I said Yes
to what life had for me,
and found myself again—
living whole and free.

Just a reminder that feeling the hurt from an old wound you thought had healed is not a setback—it's a normal part of being a beautiful, tender, loving human with feelings that ebb and flow.

Hope's Like That

It grabs you from the deepest places,
looks you square in the eye until
you can't look away,
somehow holds up a magic mirror
that shows you a glimmer of what's possible,
crouches down and lets you use it
as a stepping stool
to the dreams that are
waiting for you, and
is never ever surprised by the
heights you ascend to.

I Saw a Picture of You Today—

the one where you're in the pink dress
you bought on sale, and you thought
you might not be able to pull it off,
but your daughter loved it
and said you had to get it,
that it was meant for you.
I admit I zoomed in on your eyes and
what I saw was joy—deliberate
            and impossible.
A journey bigger, more
frayed than the fabric's
            zigzag-patterned lines,
but there you were,
smiling.
And it left me enchanted by the kind of
heart that overcomes—
tender,
strong,
otherworldly and real all at once.
What a beauty, I thought.

How long it took to speak
of me in such a way.

Glimmers

Turning the little fairy lights on after you spent the day crying / watching a sunset that takes your breath away / sharing memes that you know will make them laugh out loud / drinking from your favorite mug / resting your head on your pillow and exhaling / listening to your end-of-year playlist and sending it to the people you love / toasting a new year even amidst uncertainty / reading your favorite poem / loving yourself through everything.

Thank you for being my human glimmer.

She Found Joy Again

and it embraced her like a long-lost friend.
She didn't think it would ever return,
but it was patiently waiting for her
with healing and grace and strength to endure.
The truth is it never left,
it was just overshadowed by sorrow—
still it stayed by her side with arms open wide,
hopeful, expectant, for a better tomorrow.

You don't have to figure it all out today. The same wisdom and intuition that has guided you again and again is right here with you in this moment. You've already made it through your lowest days, and your strength and courage are forces that can't be diminished, no matter how uncertain life may feel. You are worthy of rest, peace, and presence, even when the way forward seems unclear. You'll know what to do, one step at a time and one breath at a time. You've got this, beautiful friend.

I hope you know how brave it is
to stand in your own power
to reclaim joy and wonder as a birthright
to hold the truth close to your chest
          undeterred by the turbulence around you
to evolve
to revolt
to wander in forests
          and rewrite your story
to notice how the birds spread their wings and soar
to laugh until you cry
to wear the stunning layers of your heart proudly
to heal over and over
to feel everything you need to.

On the Days When I Doubt, Love Still Finds Me

Today I'm struggling with manifestation,
three wishes and a magic lamp,
conjuring up outcomes with the sheer power of my mind
takes more belief than I can find.
But I do know
I dreamed of you
a thousand lifetimes ago
in a supernova sleep
surrounded by swirling galaxies—
and I do know
today
that's all I need.

The Best Kind of Plot Twist

Maybe you've had to put your guard up,
to expect the worst,
to protect yourself and your tender heart
after the hurt and trauma.
But what if there's a plot twist coming,
and it's the way life surprises you with all of its goodness?
What if after heartbreak,
there's love that heals you?
What if after disappointment,
there are new dreams to be fulfilled?
What if after so many tears,
there's laughter—
the kind that gets deep in your bones and echoes after?
What if after confusion,
there's wisdom—the gold you gleaned from circumstances
you should never have had to go through?
What if after loneliness,
there's connection—with others who know pain intimately
but who, like you, didn't let it harden them?
What if after self-doubt and shattered confidence,
there's self-love and assurance
that is so fortified within you it can't be shaken or taken
from you?

If you can't find hope or joy right now, may you feel the whisper of *what-if*, and may it give you the strength to keep going.

In case no one told you today,
your capacity to love,
to feel,
to evolve,
and to heal,
is beautiful, sacred, and something to be proud of.

The Parts of You That Deserve Unconditional Love

All of your uncertainty
and the fear that no one else sees

the part of you that feels unsure
and the five-year-old you once were

the mountains you've so bravely climbed
and the moments you wish you could rewind

the part of you that's still learning to love yourself
and each heartbreaking disappointment you've felt

your future and endless possibilities
and your big, beautiful, audacious dreams

your light, your shadow, your essence, your soul,
your past and your present, your highs and your lows

when you love every facet, you build love for the whole—
a love for the ages that deepens and grows.

I hope you give yourself grace to grow, to learn, to fail, and to be human.

Some things happen in this lifetime that cause you deep pain and heartache you never deserved and never should have had to go through, and there is no hidden meaning that could possibly make everything feel better. But I do believe nothing is wasted—not your tears or your sleepless nights, not your heartache or the quiet burdens you carry that no one else sees. Because when I look at you, I see your courage and your beauty, after everything. I see the strength that brought you here and the depths of your compassion and the fierceness of your spirit. I see the way you make this world a better place. *And I hope today you see it too.*

Reminders of How Much You've Grown

You've stayed true to who you are in a world that's constantly telling you what you need to change.

You've dared to keep dreaming when disappointment told you to give up.

You've done the work of healing even when it would have been easier to stay stuck in a cycle of fear.

You've kept your heart open to love even when it would have felt safer to put walls up to protect yourself from more hurt.

You've welcomed in moments of joy and reminded yourself how deserving you are to feel every bit of it.

You've taken the higher road even when it would have felt satisfying to match their energy in the moment.

You've listened to your body and rested without apology or justification.

You've lost all interest in the impossibility of perfectionism and chosen authenticity instead.

You've allowed lightness and ease into your life instead of tying everything to productivity and successful outcomes.

You've deepened your connections to the people who give you unconditional belonging and the space to be who you are.

Relearning Her ABCs

Once upon a time, she chose to be
authentic instead of agreeable,
bold instead of boxed-in, and
courageous instead of courteous. She
dove into life even when she felt afraid, and
everything changed. She
found freedom after all she'd
gone through, and although she'd been to
hell and back, she discovered peace
in ways she never imagined and
joy she never thought was possible. She
knew that every
little step she took mattered, and that the
magic in her soul could
not be taken from her. She went
on to claim her
power, no longer
questioning her worth. She learned to
rest, finding solace in
sunsets, and hope in
the night sky. She gained a deeper
understanding of her unwavering
value, and she began to dream
without limits. If you
x-rayed her heart,
you would see scars that healed, and if you
zoomed in, you would see love in every molecule.

It's Only a Matter of Time Until

You see how things were working out for you behind the scenes.

The heartbreaking disappointment you feel right now turns into a celebration that something more aligned came along.

The unhealed parts of you transform into wisdom and guidance for someone else who needs to hear your story.

The consistency you're using to reach your dreams pays off in ways that will amaze you.

III.

LIGHT THAT CANNOT BE TAKEN

Remember those days you thought you'd never get through?

But then you found the strength to overcome.

Remember the things that scared you?

But then you found the courage to take another step.

Remember the loneliness you felt in your lowest moments?

But then you found the love within you.

Remember when they tried to dim your light?

But then you remembered that nothing could stop you from shining bright.

That same strength, courage, love, and light is within you today, for whatever you're facing.

It has never left you, and it never will.

The responsibility of healing from wounds you should never have had to endure can feel heavy, unfair, and overwhelming. That's why healing is brave work. Soulful work. Honest work. And just the fact that you're showing up, seeking to nurture those wounds you didn't deserve, is powerful. I hope you remember to celebrate that today.

May You Gift Yourself the Freedom

To discard the hurtful words
and jarring actions of those who were unwilling
to see you,
for reasons you don't need to understand.
To let them do their own work,
or not.
To befriend your demons.
To shine a little light on them
and rob them of their mystery and power.
To be unproductive.
To be indulgent.
To exhale.
To know who you are and stand firm
in the truth
of it.

You've survived too much to settle for anything less than you deserve / to shrink in order to make others feel more comfortable / to let self-doubt stand in the way of achieving your goals / to feel like you have to fit into the pressure of someone else's timeline / to let fear convince you that you don't have what it takes to make your dreams come true.

You are an infinite,
luminous force in the world.
And even though you've been through
the hardest times that tried to
crush you,
shrink you,
and stop you,

here you are,
shining.

I'm Just a Girl, Standing in Front of Her Reflection

asking her to love me,
to be a little more gentle
and to embrace what she sees,
to direct her gaze to all that's right
instead of what seems wrong,
to release the myth of "flawless"
and tell her she belongs,
to see her smiling eyes
full of light and stories lived,
and to pour the same love on herself
that she so freely gives.
Maybe you were just a girl
when you believed the messages they gave—
that beauty was the holy grail,
impossible to attain.
I hope next time you look at you,
a knowing overflows
and you see the stunning wonder
of your body, spirit, soul.

Yes, I'm Sure I Would Like to Unsubscribe

— from the noise telling me what I need to do,
achieve, and consume to make myself more worthy

— from the invisible, mythical timeline telling me I'm behind

— from endless distractions that pull me out of the present moment

— from the echo of their opinions on what I should do with my life when they haven't walked a day in my shoes

— from the false sense of safety I feel by not confronting my deepest fears

— from the need to be understood by those who never saw me

— from filtered highlight reels that could never eclipse the authenticity and power of being exactly who I am

— from the outrageous idea that I was ever too much, or not enough, or anything other than sovereignly, wholly me.

You will never need to shapeshift to fit in spaces
where you truly belong.

Love Her Well

I hope when you look back at your life
you can love her well,
scoop up every version of her in your arms
and tell her she did her best—
her shiny misguided ambition,
the fool she made of herself for love,
the little girl finding shapes in the clouds,
rescuing caterpillars and
building them palaces,
her honesty,
her softness,
her laugh,
her heart,
her goodness.
All of the signals and rules
and memo slips and instructions
she collected over days and decades,
telling her what a life should be,
and then
her insight to step back,
burn it all to the ground,
and *reimagine everything.*
I hope you see her for the hero she is—
tears in her cape but still flying.
I hope you hold her face in your hands
and study her like art already
deemed worthy of
exhibition.

I hope you have that kind of bias,
a silent sovereign awe
for courage personified,
covered in glorious skin,
luminous
and glistening in the sun.

Dear Eleven-Year-Old Me,

How are you doing?
How's the view from up in that tree,
what are you thinking?
I see you over there
with your arms in the air,
your gentle smile and caring eyes,
running free with the wind in your hair,
and you're chasing fireflies.
Some people will try to bring you down,
and they'll leave a few scars on your soul,
but you're never going to lose who you are
as an eleven-year-old.

Dear twenty-two-year-old me,
How are you doing?
Where did you get that uncertainty?
Stops you from moving.
I see you heartbroken
from the words that they've spoken,
you feel lost and unsure,
desperate to find the things that were stolen,
but your courage will endure.
Some people will try to bring you down,
and they'll leave a few scars on your soul,
but you're never going to lose who you are
as an eleven-year-old.

I wish I could go back in time
and wrap my arms around you.
I'd tell you it will be alright
and you have the strength to make it through,
but I know one day you'll remember
what you always knew—
that no one can stop the light that shines from you.

Dear seventy-year-old me,
How are you doing?
I hope you're dancing wild and free,
and it's still you you're choosing.

I hope you remove another layer of the burdens
placed on you that were never yours to carry.

After You, I Stopped Cloaking My Worth with a Question Mark

until it became an exclamation,
and the cracks in my heart healed
with tissue that was strong
but still tender.
You said you were irreplaceable,
and you were right.
I have never replaced that kind of coldness,
only displaced it
with a deeper sense of love
than I ever imagined.

Good Karma

The pink cloud I saw on an overcast day / the warmest message from the stranger who instantly became a friend / the northern lights in my front yard / the get-well gift that knew me perfectly / the hope they never stole from me / the love that took my breath away / the way my heart healed beyond my wildest imagination.

Sacred

Spring crept in like morning sunlight,
I searched for flowers on winding roads
and surrendered to the healing
while the sunsets soothed my soul.
Every step, I was reunited
with the parts of me that had gone—
they'd been covered by your shadow
for far too long.
And day by day I reclaimed the best of me
you tried to steal away,
and breath by breath I gained my strength
and felt your poison leave my veins.
I shed the weight of words you spoke to me
that tried to make me small.
I found power in the memory
of who I was before I knew you at all.
And you'll never take it from me,
I've learned how to protect my peace.
I'm proud to say I finally learned to love
every sacred part of me.

And when she returned to herself,
it was the most beautiful reunion.
"I've been looking for you," she said.
"I've been waiting for you," she answered.
And then
they embraced
and
never let go
again.

Did You Hear?

She alchemized their poison into stardust,
painted it pink and gold,
sprinkled it on her skin
until she was fluorescent,
until she shone in the moonlight,
until the glow was everywhere,
within her and around her,
leaving a glimmering trail behind her.
Then she wrote in neon—
a message that lit up the entire sky—
Whoever you are, wherever you are,
beautiful soul,
you belong here in this vast universe,
and you will heal,
and hope is yours,
and love is with you,
and that will always be enough.

Tuning Out the Noise

Too much, too little
too quiet, too visible
too strong, too weak
too confident, too meek
too perfect, too flawed
too big, too small
too young, too old
too timid, too bold.
Too wise to care what they think
we should be,
too busy for their judgment
being brave, fierce, and free,
knowing life's too short
for that toxic energy
and their opinions don't affect
our hard-earned destiny.
Their barometer will change
and their goalposts will move,
but liberation is remembering
we have nothing to prove.
Too focused on our dreams
to concede to their control
because our true power lies in knowing
we're already whole.

When life feels cold,
may you remember your warmth.

When life feels overwhelming,
may you remember your strength.

When life feels unclear,
may you remember your wisdom.

When life feels harsh,
may you remember your kindness.

When life feels unfair,
may you remember your goodness.

When life feels scary,
may you remember your courage.

When life feels hard,
may you remember your tenderness.

And when life feels joyful,
may you soak in every moment
and know there's so much more to come.

Once she realized
she had the courage all along,

her heart was vivacious,
resilient, and strong,

her mind was vivid
and sharp and discerning,

her ruby desires alive and burning,

she tore down the tapestry,
set herself free,

danced along the yellow brick road,

then clicked her heels
and found her way home.

One by One, the Fragments Align

You won't be able to imagine it when you're in the throes of heartache, disappointment, and derailed dreams,

but one day soon you'll laugh so loud it catches you by surprise because there was a time you thought joy had disappeared forever.

And one day soon you'll see a picture of yourself with your head held high and peace in your eyes, and you'll have to do a double-take because there was a time you shrank so much you didn't know how you'd ever be seen again.

And one day soon you'll be so present in the moment, at ease and connected, that it will bring tears to your eyes because there was a time you felt so lost you didn't know how you'd ever find yourself again.

And one day soon you'll be sharing your story in safe spaces and it's not the pain that will stand out, it's your strength, your bravery, and the way you've kept your heart tender and alive.

However shattered you may feel, please know there is a rebuilding happening, moment by moment, that will leave you nothing short of wonderstruck.

She took this reminder
wherever she went—
through valleys
through shadows
through every road's bend.
No matter what was
and whatever may be,
she is whole
she is healed
she is loved
she is free.

IV.

LIGHT THAT ILLUMINATES THE WAY FORWARD

Sometimes life whispers with a nudge toward change, growth, and momentum—*It's time to expand.* And yes, this thing you didn't think was attainable, is. Trust it. Trust you. Trust the tingling in your fingertips and the grounding in your deepest self. Trust your heart and the direction it's calling you to, even when you don't know how it will all work out.

That dream in your heart,
the one written on paper and crumpled,
carried in your worn pockets
through countless steps and storms,
the one that just won't leave,
that sketches its *what-if*
on the edges of your heart—
What if it could happen?
What if it's not too late?
What if you have what it takes?
What if the stars are aligned this time?
What if you learned what you needed to?
What if your hard-won wisdom is the fuel?
What if, as you've widened the capacity
        in your life for possibility,
        there's just no more room for regret?
What if I told you I believe in you?

What if you believe in you too?

Fear will try to convince you that you need certainty in order to move forward.

Courage knows that taking another step, even in uncertainty, can reveal the most beautiful path.

Heartache will try to convince you that the pain will never go away.

Healing knows that however fragmented you feel, things are stitching together day by day and breath by breath.

Disappointment will try to convince you that what you're dreaming of is out of reach.

Hope knows that you are closer than ever to the future you're pursuing.

Self-doubt will try to convince you that you're stuck where you are.

Inner wisdom knows that no matter the ups and downs of life, you have what it takes to keep stepping into all that's meant for you.

Off the Charts

All of the flip charts and pie charts
and graphs and formulas and algorithms
can't tell you the most important thing
you need to know—
that you hold unconditional value
beyond all validation,
that you top the tables
with your unique light,
that the exact blueprint only you hold,
technically etched in your DNA,
wondrously written across galaxies,
is enough.
Enough permission for you
to chase your dreams with unapologetic audacity.
Enough strength to hold your head high
at every single table and in every single room.
Enough momentum to propel you
to the life you desire.
Enough love to heal the places you thought
healing would never find.
Enough peace to know
in this microsecond of a moment
that all you are,
all of you,
is indisputably, immeasurably worthy.

You can feel it when it's time to shed another layer.
Your skin becomes uncomfortable and ill-fitting.
I'm always a little afraid at first.
I'm not sure what the new skin will feel like—
will it be too obvious, shiny, on display?
Will I long for what's been?
But then I remember
everything it took to bring me to this moment,
all of the letting go
that gave me room to grow and hope and dream.
So I close my eyes,
watch the old float away,
and trust the new.

In case no one told you today,
the way you keep choosing courage over fear is
inspiring.

To the One Who Is in a Season of Unknowns,

I know that having the answers, or a crystal ball to see how it all works out, would bring comfort in this moment. And you deserve to feel comforted. But I hope you know that in this time of uncertainty, there are many certain truths:

how you've already overcome some of your hardest days with a strength and bravery that others would marvel at

how the love and light that lives within you can't ever be diminished by what you're going through

how there are memories to be made that you can't imagine right now

how there are doors to be opened, no matter how many have closed before

how there is belonging to be found, after all of the times you've felt alone

how alignment happens and good things take root and foundations are formed even when you can't see it yet

and how much this world needs you, your gifts, your experience, and your wisdom, not because of the pain *but because you were brave.*

There's a Future Version of You That's So Proud

that you didn't give up in your hardest moments

of the work you're putting in behind the scenes

that you're choosing hope even when you feel overwhelmed and
afraid

of the love, care, and compassion you're learning to give yourself

and that you're trusting your journey and surrendering to
what's beyond your control.

There's a future version of you that's waiting with open arms,
and cheering for you every step of the way.

Trust Your Intuition, Wise Soul

Heart decisions
aren't about polished precision,
external recognition,
perfection
or endless introspection—
they are
life flowing, gut knowing,
chest pounding, love abounding,
have-to-do-this
or at least have to try,
and if I fall
or if I fly,
I'll keep on following
that wisdom inside
(because I don't want to carry
regret through my life).

I hope today you remember

to be kind to you too,

to love each facet of you,

to know you're doing the best you can do,

to celebrate everything you've made it through,

to believe your wildest dreams can come true.

Sometimes you have to crack your heart wide open
again
even when you feel like hurt
is the only thing you've known.
Sometimes you have to close your eyes,
take the leap, and let the momentum
of all that you are carry you forward.
Sometimes you have to breathe,
and sometimes you have to hold your breath
with the maddening uncertainty of outcomes.
Sometimes you have to embrace the madness,
the messiness,
and recklessly expand the lines you once drew in,
because the life that's calling to you
can't wait for you to see what happens next.

This Is the Part Where

all of your hard work pays off and doors open in unexpected ways

you come back wiser, stronger, and more compassionate after all you've been through

the redirection leads you to the most beautiful places

your sense of self-worth becomes so powerful that you shine from the inside out

your inner peace is the glow-up they can't stop talking about

you enter rooms and sit at tables you've been dreaming of

you know that rest, softness, and ease are not deterrents to your goals, but help you achieve them

your biggest flex is realizing you have nothing to prove to anyone but you

your loudest cheerleaders are your past self and your future self that are both so proud of how far you've come

To the one wondering
if they deserve the good things
happening right now
when you've grown
so accustomed to struggle,
you do
you do
you do.
Pain and healing taught you
but now joy is waiting for you.

Just a reminder that no one else has to understand your dreams, your decisions, your plans, or your life to make them any more valid, beautiful, and worthy of pursuing.

It's easy to mistake fear for a guiding voice on your path (for example, a reason to stay where you are, to not take action or go after the dream that terrifies you). Your body is hardwired to honor fear and listen to it as the loudest voice, in order to protect you. But there's a deeper, steadier voice inside of you that knows it's okay to be afraid *and* do the thing your heart is calling you to. The goal isn't to be rid of fear, the goal is to trust the wiser knowing within you. *It takes real courage to let love be louder than fear.*

I Hope Today You Measure Your Success By

— the way you've kept showing up, even when you were afraid

— the compassion and kindness you've learned to give yourself for your struggles

— the courage it's taken to overcome challenges and setbacks

— the times you've gotten back up again when life knocked you down

— the wisdom you've used to grow and evolve

— the determination and consistency you've had to pursue your dreams

— the hope you keep holding on to, even when it all feels overwhelming

I hope you remember that success is much more than surface-level. It's the behind-the-scenes, beautiful journey you're on and the brave steps you're taking along the way.

Don't mistake her kindness for weakness—
she's been through the darkest valleys,
and her ability to remain soft is deliberate and battle-won.

Don't mistake her optimism for naivety—
she embraces both the light and the shadows
and has learned to love herself every step of the way.

Don't mistake her silence for defeat—
she's learned where to invest her energy
and when to choose her peace over proving herself
to anyone else.

Don't mistake her tears for despair—
she's learned to feel her feelings unapologetically
and to give herself compassion on her hardest days.

Don't mistake her dreams for delusions—
she's shattering glass ceilings, and she's only just getting started.

Inner Peace

She's standing on the sand
with the wind in her hair
she's breathing in the calm
the oxygen and air
she's looking at the sun
and it's embracing her with light
she's watching as the birds
sing their song in flight
she thinks of all she burned to ash
and all she left behind
and instead of sinking from the weight
she knows her power this time—
fierce and tender
in gentle surrender
with love that bursts from every scar
brave, afraid
she wouldn't trade
the truth and hope held in her heart.

And she lived authentically ever after.

Profit and Loss (Soul Edition)

You lost the fear that kept you frozen,
    and you gained adventure.
You lost the self-doubt that tried to stop you,
    and you gained freedom.
You lost acquaintances,
    and you gained true friends.
You lost the things that held you back,
    and you gained possibilities
    and dreams come true.
You lost tears, sleep, composure, certainty,
    and you gained wisdom, ferocity,
    softness, surrender.
You lost an old way of thinking,
    and you gained new perspective
    and insight.
You lost layers upon layers,
    and you gained something more true
    and aligned with who you are.
And through it all, you never lost
your humanity,
your beating heart
and vibrant spirit,
your beauty
or your light.

Out with the Old, in with the . . .

ancient wisdom of my great-grandmother, who found the courage to begin again

wonder of my inner child, who learned her biggest lessons from wildflowers

laughter of my children, who followed the direction of their hearts

strength I found to move forward into possibility

gold I collected in the valleys of my lowest moments

and hope for the future that waits with open arms.

She made something new—
stunning, brave,
boundless, and true,
and they'll never be able
to take it away.
Her beautiful heart
was always here to stay.

It Turns Out, My Fairy Godmother Was Me from the Future

telling me I wouldn't be
heartbroken and hidden forever,
telling me, You've got this, my love,
we will make it through this—
just you wait and see
how the story unfolds.
You're already magical, you know it,
but this is the part where you finally
step into your goddamn power.
Then she handed me my custom shoes,
sprinkled me with courage,
and sent me riding into the night.

Maybe the Next Chapter Is About

seeing all of the seeds you've planted flourish beyond your wildest imagination

following your heart and trusting your intuition

deepening connections with the people who embody love and compassion

giving yourself permission to find joy and notice the glimmers all around you

remembering that confidence is more than a feeling—it's aligned action and brave, consistent steps

honoring every part of your journey and celebrating how far you've come

watching your dreams become a reality, and inspiring others to dream too.

There are so many more beautiful chapters of your life to be written.

V.

LIGHT THAT IGNITES OTHER LIGHTS

The real win is being a safe presence for others to share their vulnerability and their fear.

What If You Are Your Epiphany?

What if the elusive spark you've been chasing—
the purpose,
the clarity,
the illumination—
is the realization that you
are incredibly worthy,
deserving of love,
and needed on this earth?
What if in this revelation of self-love
you were able to spread your light
to someone who needs this epiphany too?

Cheers To:

the healers who have taken their pain and turned it into wisdom to help others

the dreamers who are pushing the limits of what they thought was possible

the fighters who overcome battles every day that no one else sees

the tender hearts who use their softness to heal the world

the resters who know that their worth is not dependent on their productivity

the adventurers who aren't afraid of uncertainty

the creators who magically weave beauty into ordinary moments

the lighthouses who make sure no one else gets lost in the dark

The ache and beauty of hope is that it is needed the most when it's under the biggest threat, when its flame dwindles under the enormity of fear. That's when you dig deeper into your tender heart and find the embers that have carried you through impossibility before. That's when you look for the sparks of light all around you, in other tender hearts who are digging deeper too.

Kindred Spirits

I knew it straightaway.
There was a gentleness about you
that felt like a lighthouse,
like an invitation,
like a knowing,
with warm eyes that told stories,
and an essence like thunder.
And somehow your presence
felt like a permission slip,
like every light was green,
that said I see you
and Yes to the fullness of you
and Nothing amazing you do
could ever surprise me because
I already know it, that these cardboard
walls they surrounded you with are weak
and flimsy and faded.
Let's stomp them down together,
and at sunset we'll rest
and revel in the wild hope of tomorrow.

Rooting for You

If I could
I would carry your dreams for you
when your grip feels weak.
I'd hold up a mirror
and remind you that you are *radiant.*
Then I'd take the hopes in your heart,
write them in the sky,
set off fireworks,
and celebrate with you when
they come to pass.
And all that is to say
I believe in you,
and when you forget who you are
and what you're capable of,
I will remind you
in a thousand undeniable ways.

I Can't Wait for the Part of Your Story Where

You understand a little more why that thing you really wanted didn't work out.

You amaze yourself with how much you've healed.

You notice the progress from all of the work you're putting in behind the scenes.

You see all of the love you've given make its way back to you.

That obstacle you never thought you'd overcome becomes a small object in the rearview mirror.

You give yourself so much grace to be human that perfectionism can't sabotage your progress no matter how hard it tries.

Your most noticeable wins are the self-love and self-compassion you cultivated even when you felt lost and afraid.

You share the wisdom you've gained through your challenges with someone else who needs to know they're not alone.

I can't wait for the part of your story where
that dream on your vision board
becomes a lived moment on your camera roll.

To the Beautiful Friend Who Doesn't Realize Their Impact

Your courage is inspiring—
the way you choose again and again
to grow, to risk, to dream,
the way you've risen above your hurts,
refusing to let them define you,
the way you keep spreading your light,
and the way you bravely wear your softness,
refuse walls and facade,
and choose love every time.
I want you to know how much
I admire the person you are,
who you've always been,
and who you're becoming every day.

I hope you believe in yourself so much that other people start believing in themselves just by watching you.

The Search Is Over

I looked for a world
with flowers in bloom,
where the sun would ignite
and dance with the moon,
where there'd only be peace
and just oceans of truth,
but most of all,
I looked for you.

I looked for the stars
that would shine in the night,
where warmth would radiate
in sound and in sight,
where love would rise up
to the highest of heights,
but most of all,
I looked for your light.

I looked for a drop—
what I found was the sea,
a miraculous journey
that brought you to me,
the cosmos aligned
with vast galaxies,
for most of all,
we were meant to be.

There Are Thirty Trillion Cells in Your Body

Thirty trillion proofs of life.
Thirty trillion chances to shed and evolve.
Thirty trillion expressions of being.
Thirty trillion dreams in the making.
Thirty trillion reasons to love you.
Thirty trillion accidentless existences.
Thirty trillion revolutions and resurrections.
And if I have to tell you thirty trillion ways
that you matter,
that you light up the sky with your
molecular magnitude,
that we need you here,
then I'll spend thirty trillion lifetimes
to say it is so.

Architects of Belonging

It doesn't always feel true
that we're the architects of our
own happiness.
We lose and we grieve and we
crawl in valleys so dark
our eyes dim and then burn in the sun.
We try to make sense, find meaning,
control what we can, and then painfully come
to the realization of all that's beyond our control.
And if impermeable joy is an elusive goal,
maybe instead our lives are just supposed to be
spacious—
with enough room for every speck of our humanity,
our light and our shadows,
with enough courage and wonder
to build something more lasting than joy alone—
a safe place for all—
for heartbreak and for laughter,
for dancing and feeling
and being.
Maybe our lives are simply meant to be
a refuge that says,
Your truest self will be honored here,
you can sit here,
I love you.

The way you believed in me
when I couldn't find the strength
to believe in me too
skyrocketed me to universes I only ever dreamed of.

Your Life Is Not a Performance Review

with graphs and stats and endless numbers.
There are no awards for never rested,
never made a mistake,
never fell flat on your face in the middle of the race,
never wished you'd been softer in a moment,
never wished you'd been fiercer in a moment,
never ruffled any feathers,
never disliked by anyone,
never blew off plans to walk barefoot by the ocean,
never had the triple-scoop ice cream
          even when you were full from pizza,
never asked for help,
never cried until your eyes stopped generating tears,
never risked it all for the pursuit of what's true,
never ached, never desired, never dreamed of impossible things.
Mostly, the legacy you leave will be
your beauty in the eyes of the people who saw you
and the people you saw too.
Mostly, it will have nothing to do with performance
or perfection or conventional success,
and everything to do with the love and compassion
you gave and received
and the wonder you chose to notice—
the awe you felt for a messy world asking to be inhaled
like your very breath depended on it.

Flying Lessons

I hope you remember that every detour you've taken
and each moment you felt alone
and all the times your best plans were shaken
and you couldn't see how you'd grown,
and the moments of darkness you walked through
and the days the sun disappeared,
when the clouds almost engulfed you
and you felt overwhelmed by your fears—
they never stopped your good heart from shining,
your courage kept finding a way.
Even then, the stars were aligning,
guiding you to a much brighter day,
and now you're *here* breathing in deeply;
you found peace after the storm,
giving yourself to life completely,
looking forward to all that's in store.
Knowing that every step you take matters
and nothing can put out your light,
and when everything seemed to shatter,
dear friend, *that's when you learned to fly.*

You're a Mirror of Light

All of those battles only you know about—
the tears, the sweat, and the pain,

all of those steps you took
and the moments you felt alone and afraid,

all of those times you refused to let hurt harden you,
when you chose to show compassion anyway,

all of the work you've done to heal
and the growth you've embraced day by day,

all of the obstacles you climbed over
and the mountains and valleys you overcame,

all of the dreams you held on to
and the hope you never let slip away,

all these things form the magic inside you—
the love and the courage you radiate.

Forged in the fire and built from the ashes,
you bravely made beauty out of your pain.

Now you hold up a mirror for others to see
their light and their worth when they forget,

reminding them that they're not alone
and sharing this truth: *There's so much more yet.*

There's something beautiful about the way you want
to make this world a better place.

It Can Happen Out of Nowhere

Suddenly, a door opens that felt like it was closed so tight it was impossible to walk through.

Suddenly, a connection happens, and the synchronicity of the separate paths that led you to each other feels nothing short of miraculous.

Suddenly, a wound heals that you thought would never mend.

Suddenly, the things that are supposed to make sense do, and you feel empowered to surrender the need to understand the things that aren't necessary to move forward.

Suddenly, small sparks of joy grow where sorrow used to reside.

Suddenly, there's peace and calm and contentment in the garden of your life that you've cultivated with a thousand small steps along the way.

Suddenly, a vision on your board that felt so out of reach you almost didn't let yourself imagine it, becomes a stunning reality.

Suddenly, the stars align and you understand the journey that brought you here with a clarity and gratitude that takes your breath away.

Suddenly, you barely recognize this version of you and your life, and yet it's undeniably familiar because the beautiful soul that's guided you is evergreen.

Suddenly, all of the hard work, the behind-the-scenes consistency, the uncompromising determination, the growth, the compassion, and the love you never lost, translate into all you hoped for.

Suddenly, your arms are wide open to receive it all.

For the Healers Who Healed Themselves First

No matter how many times they underestimated you,
hurt you, or discounted you,
you *knew* you had what it took.
You had the courage to go after your dreams,
no matter how many setbacks you faced.
And now here you are,
standing on the fortitude of your effort,
your bravery,
the alignment of the universe,
and the kindness of strangers who didn't need
your backstory to see how brightly you shine.
Here you are, paying it forward to someone else
who's in the valley right now and can't see their way out.
Because you will never forget how it feels,
because you promised yourself
if you ever came out of that tunnel,
you would shine the brightest light you could find
to remind people there's hope.
And so it goes,
one light ignites another, and another,
until the sky is glowing with all that's meant to be.

Acknowledgments

Thank you to you, reader, for the time you've spent with this book.

Thank you to my husband Dave—for your hundreds of *Braveheart* speeches and unwavering belief in me. The universe knew that a rugby-playing, Shakespeare-buff drummer who writes love letters on Post-its was my soulmate. I love you and the life we've built together. To my son Benj and daughter Daisy—you are my heartbeat, my joy, and my endless inspiration.

Thank you to my publisher Michelle Halket for being such a kind and knowledgeable champion of authors, poetry, and the arts, and to the rest of the team at Central Avenue Publishing for seeing and supporting my work.

Thank you to my family—to my mom for your infinite love, encouragement, and support. To my dad for our deep conversations about life, and for the way you listen and care. I love you both so much. To my grandparents, whose memory will always live on. And to Kate—I'm so glad we're family.

Thank you to the lighthouses and mentors in my life: Mr. H, Judy, and Ian—you've impacted me more than words can say.

And thank you to my online community at Dear Beautiful Friend—you inspire me every day with your courage, your light, and your hope.

Photo: Sara Zarrella

Sara Christiansen Jeffs is a writer and Positive Psychology Coach and Educator (NBC-HWC). Her work brings together positive psychology, emotional intelligence, and self-love—helping people step into their next chapter with more joy, confidence, and clarity. She is the founder of @dearbeautifulfriend on Instagram and lives in New England with her family.